PIANO SOLOS

Richard Clayderman

A Romantic Christmas

HAL•LEONARD®
CORPORATION
7777 W. BLUEMOUND RD. P.O. BOX 13819 MILWAUKEE, WI 53213

Richard Clayderman
A Romantic Christmas

Contents

Ave Maria

SCHUBERT
Adaption and Arrangement by OLIVIER TOUSSAINT
and GERARD SALESSES

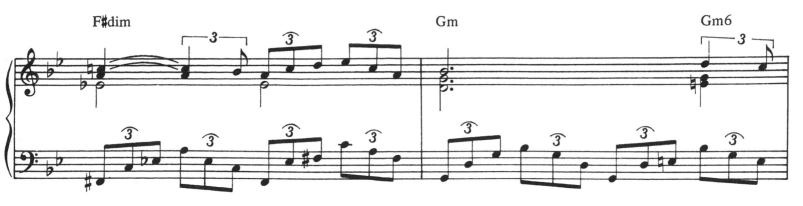

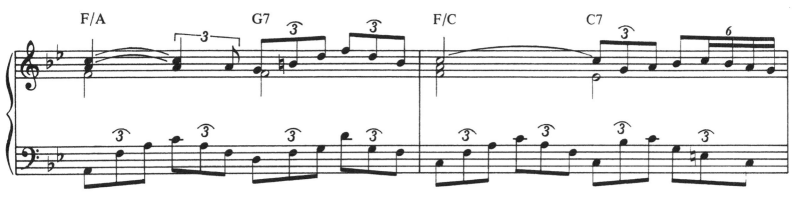

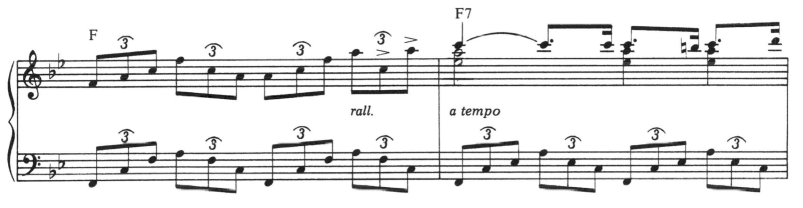

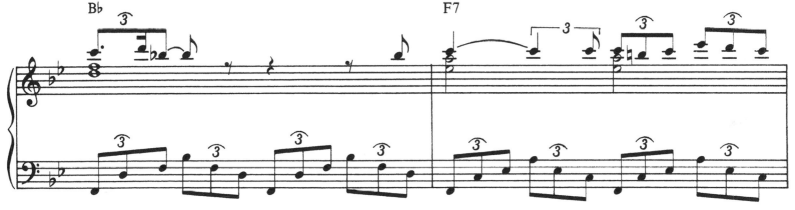

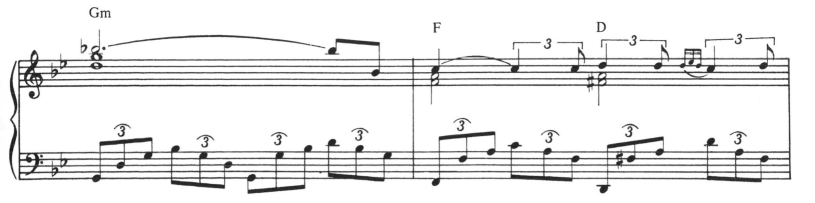

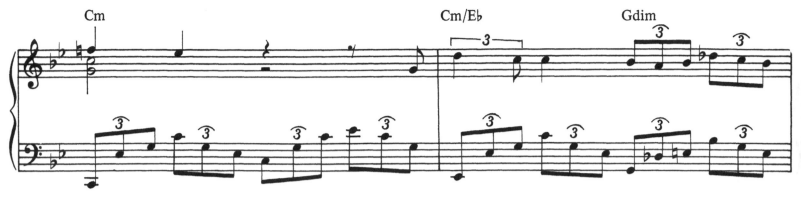

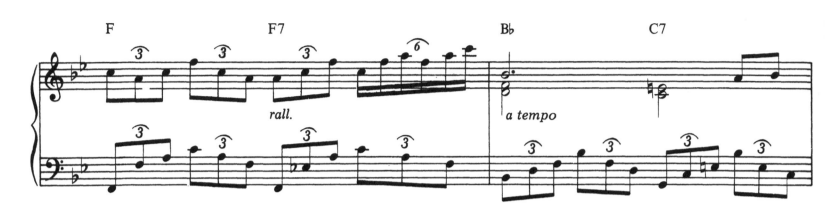

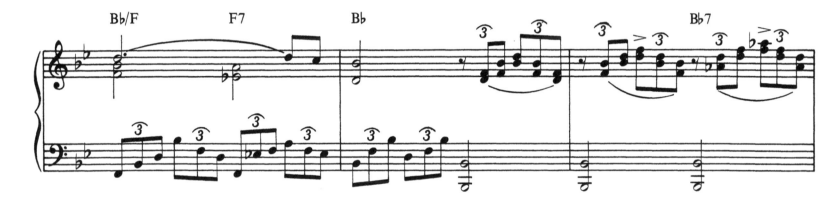

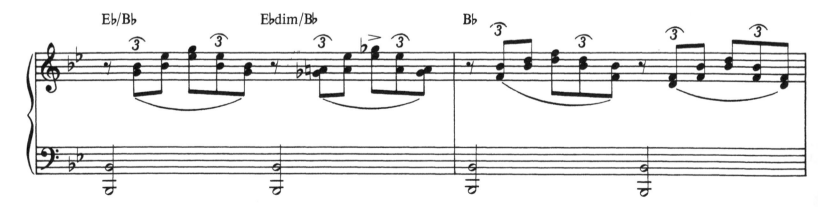

Christmas Concerto

CORELLI
Adaption and Arrangement by OLIVIER TOUSSAINT
and GERARD SALESSES

Moderately

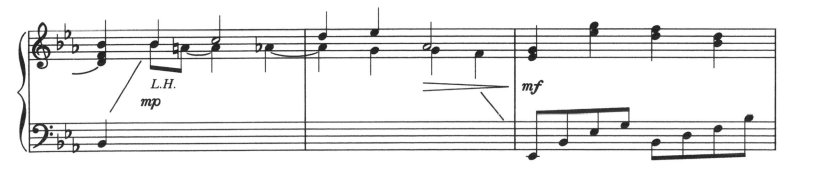

Allegro ♩ = ♩

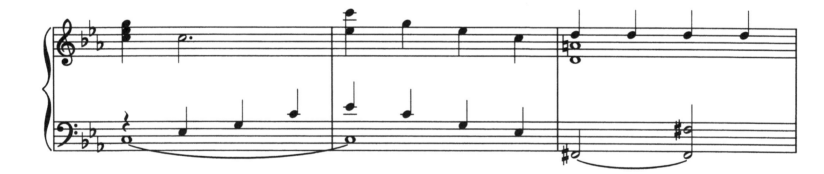

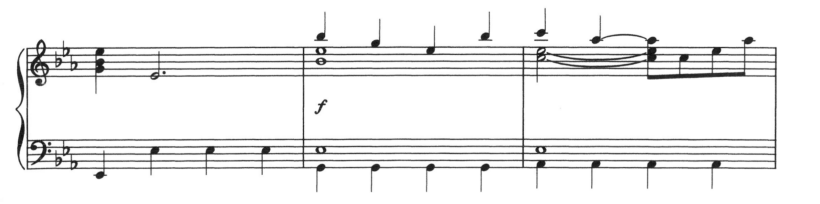

Slower

Allegro

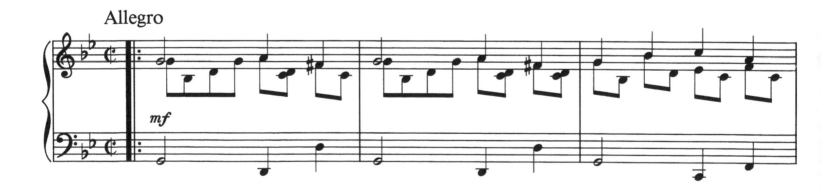

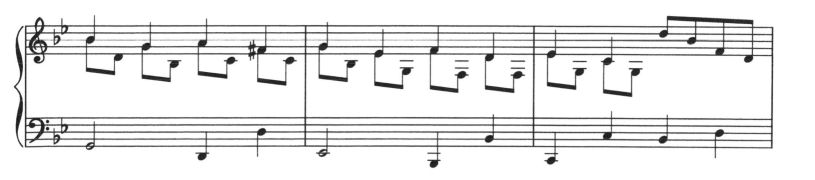

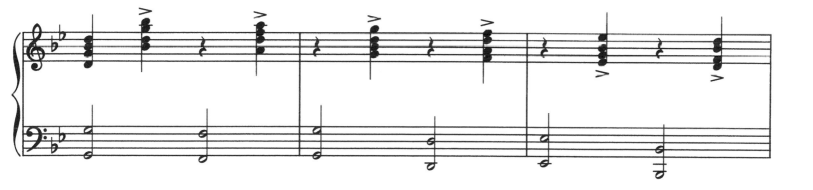

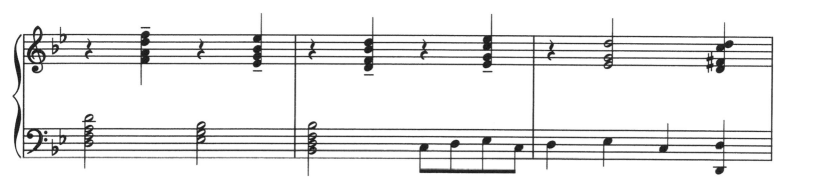

Jingle Bells

TRADITIONAL
Adaption and Arrangement by OLIVIER TOUSSAINT
and GERARD SALESSES

Moderately

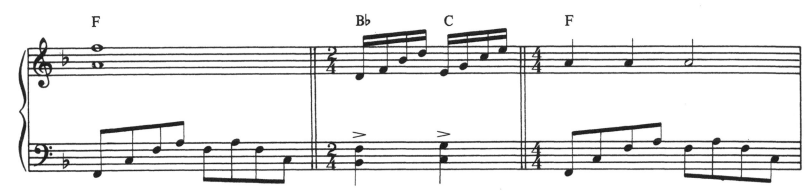

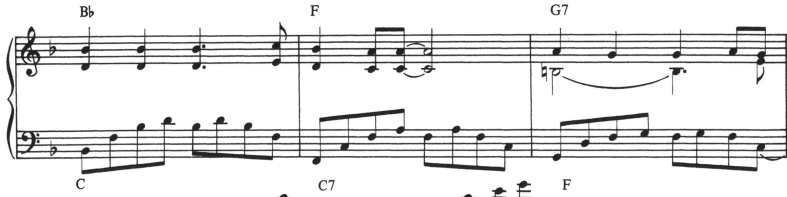

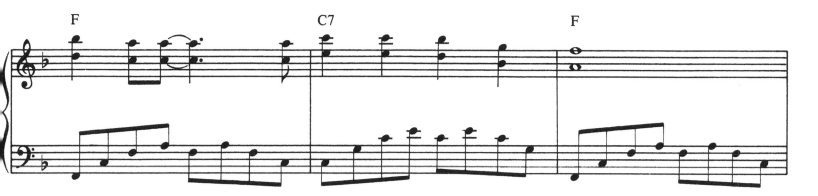

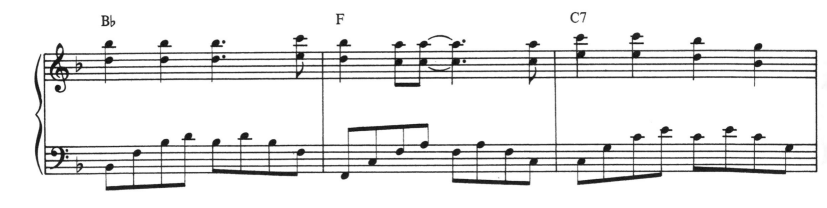

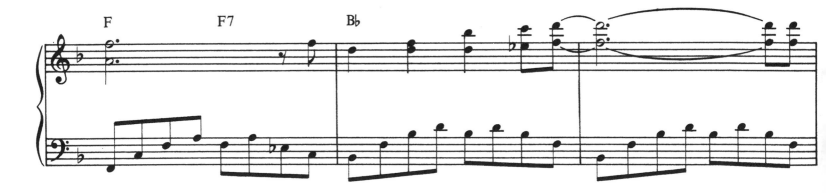

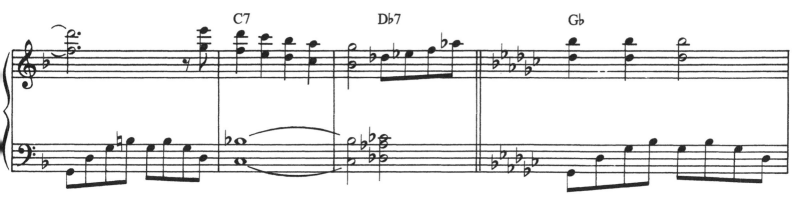

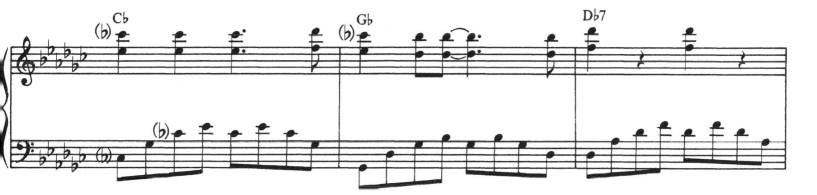

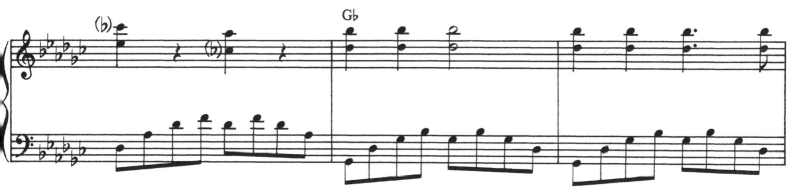

The Little Drummer Boy

By KATHERINE K. DAVIS
HENRY ONORATI and HARRY SIMEONE

8 bassa

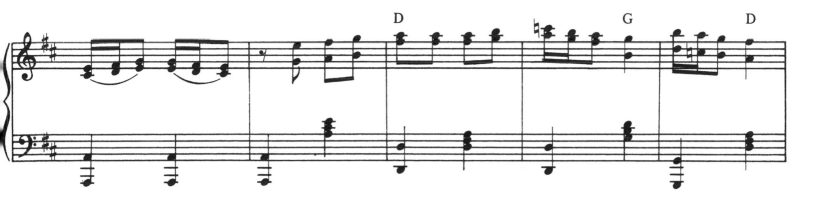

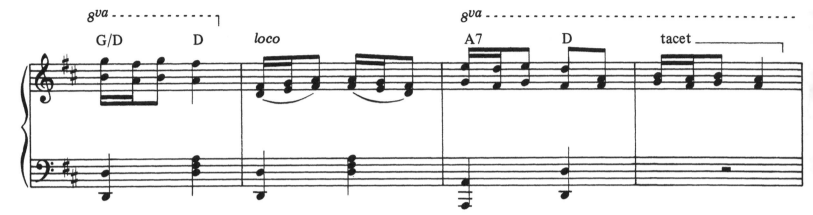

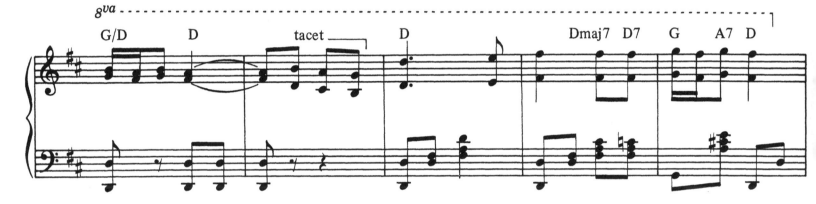

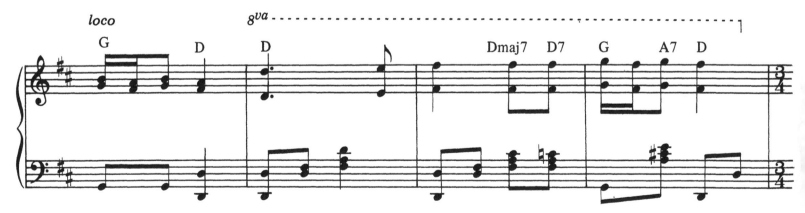

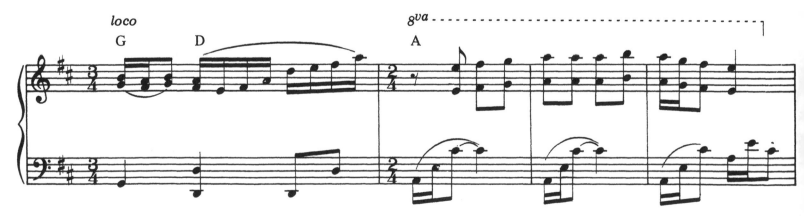

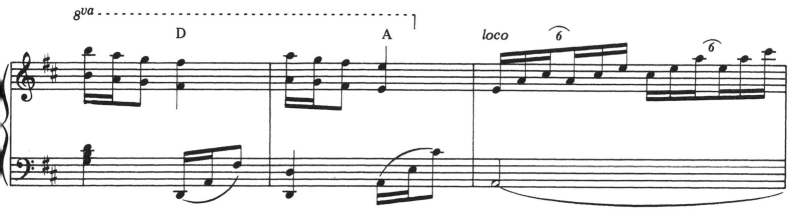

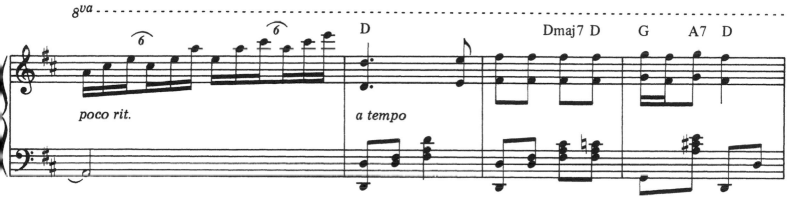

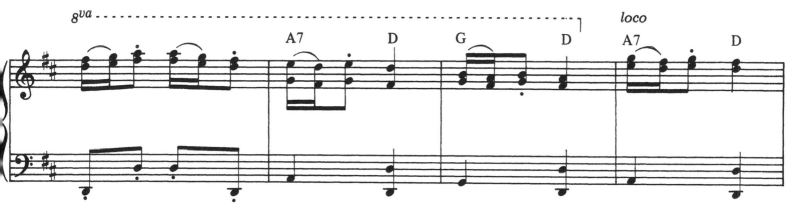

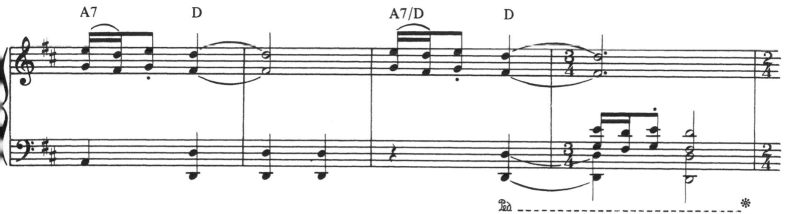

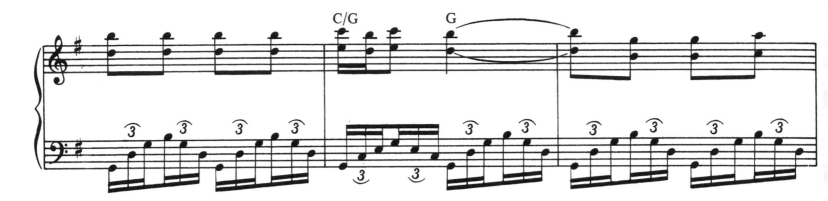

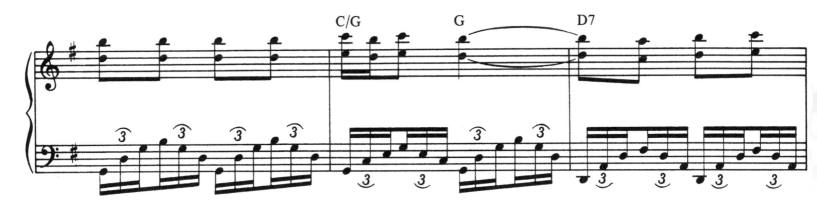

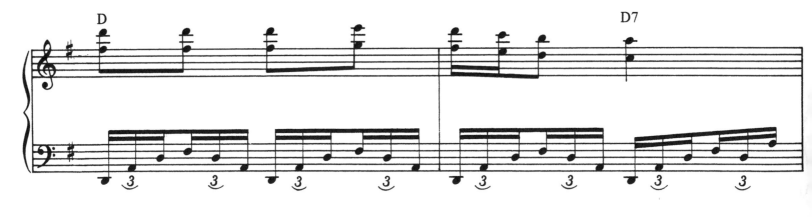

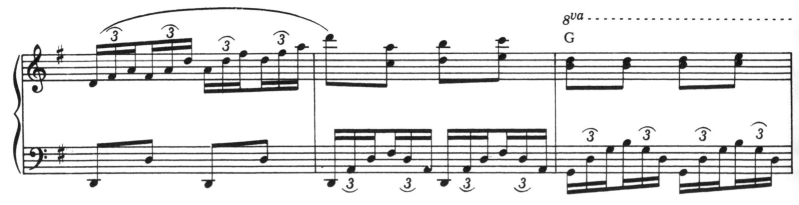

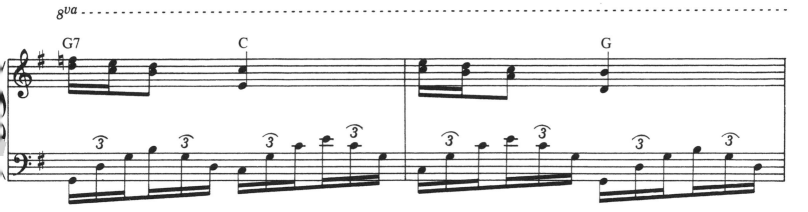

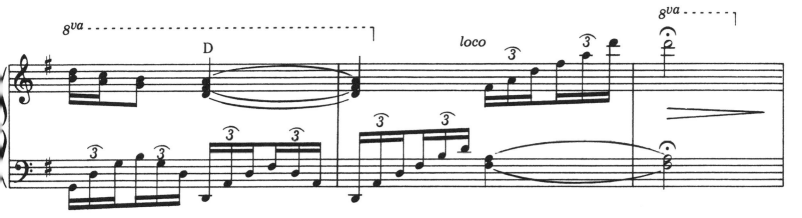

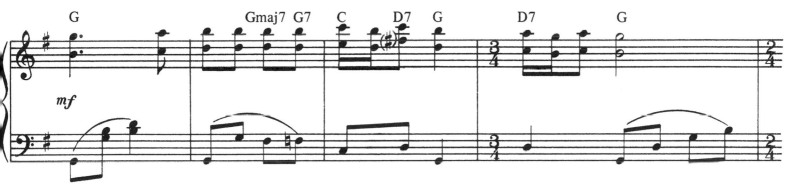

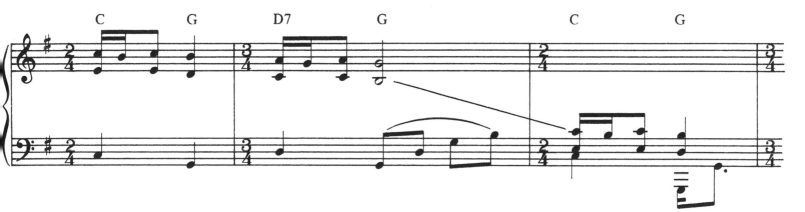

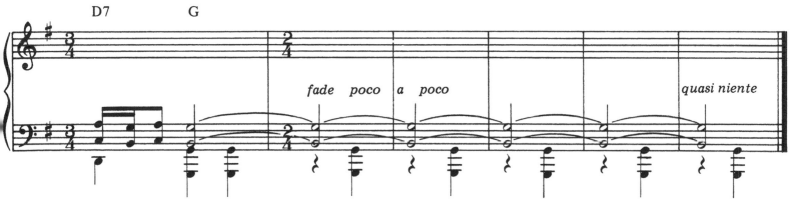

O Tannenbaum Medley

TRADITIONAL
Adaption and Arrangement by OLIVIER TOUSSAINT
and GERARD SALESSES

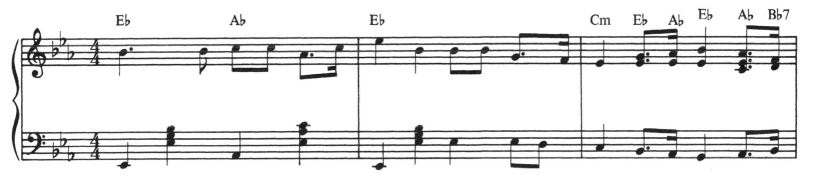

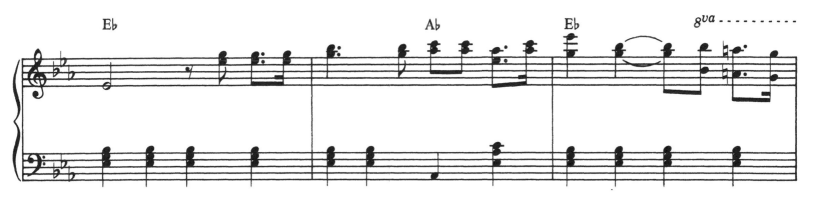

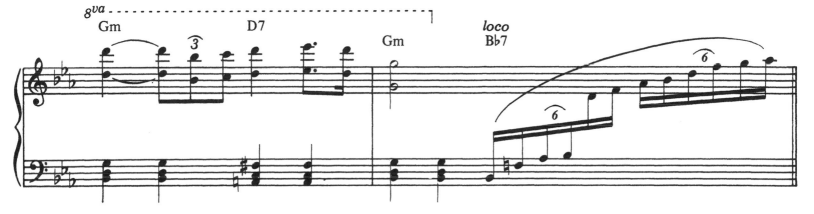

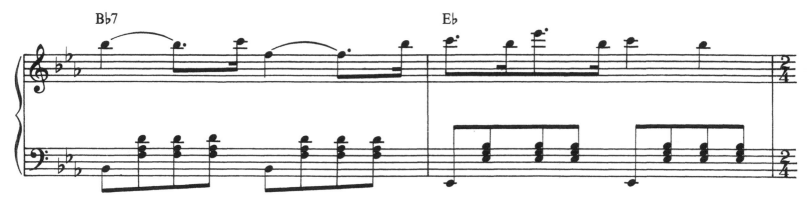

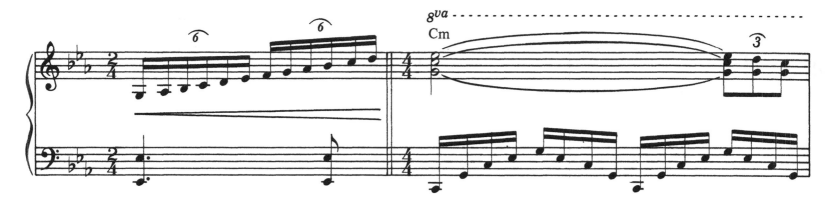

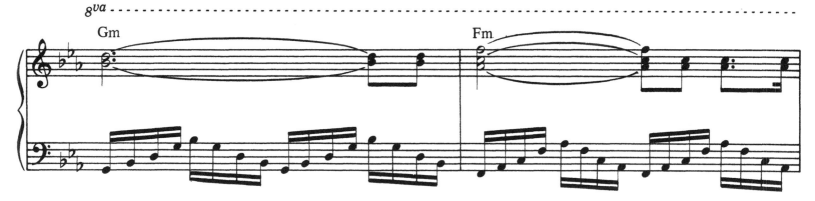

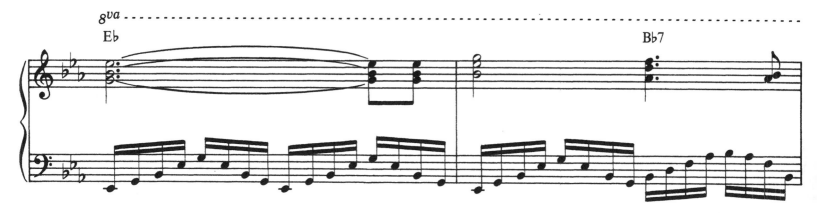

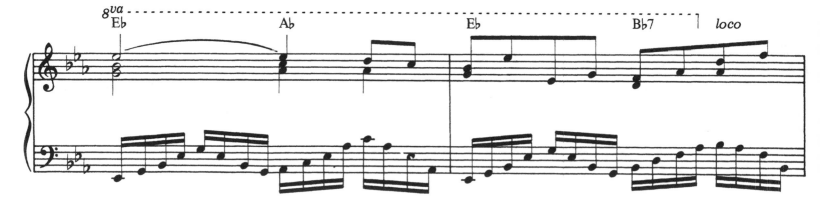

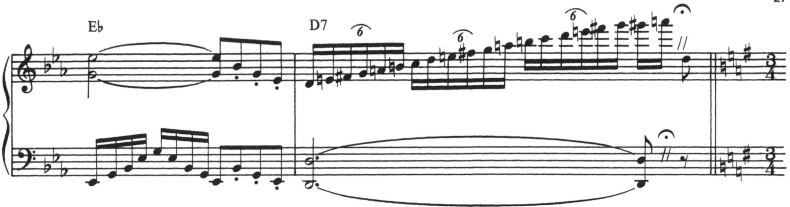

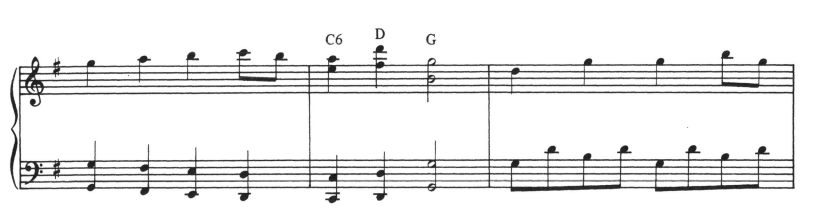

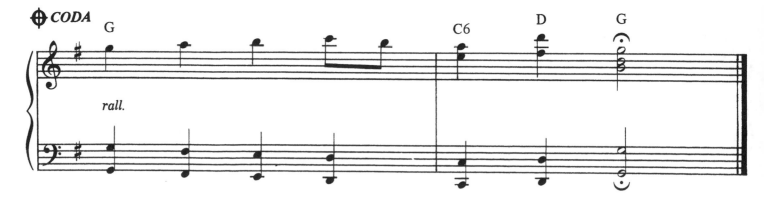

Santa Claus Is Coming To Town

Words by HAVEN GILLESPIE
Music by J. FRED COOTS

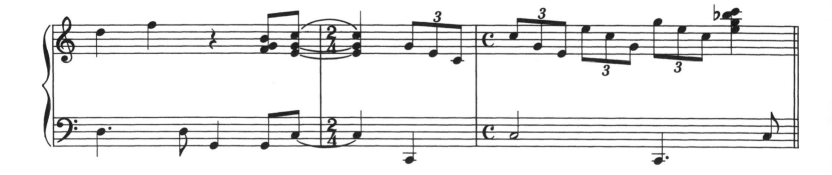

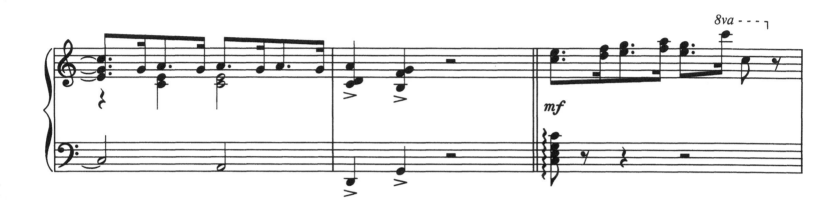

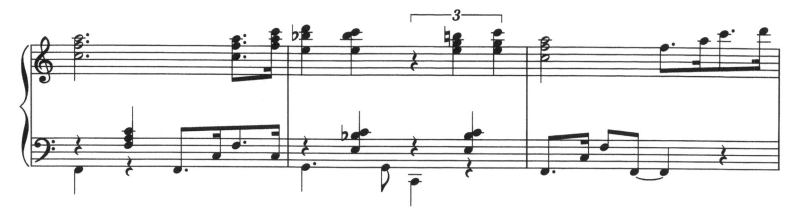

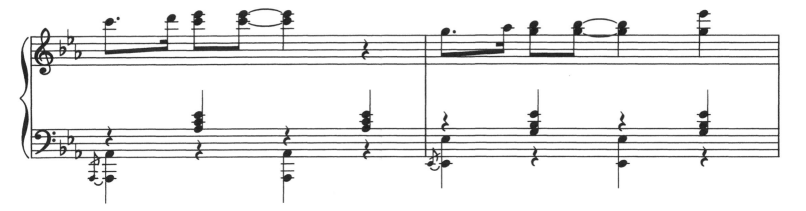

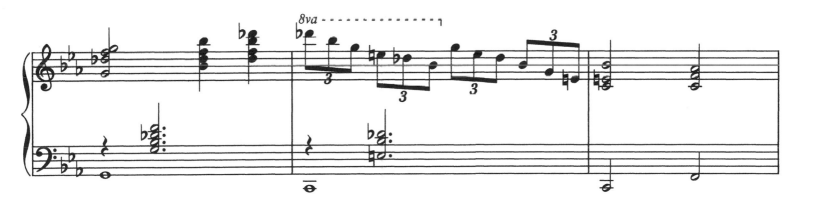

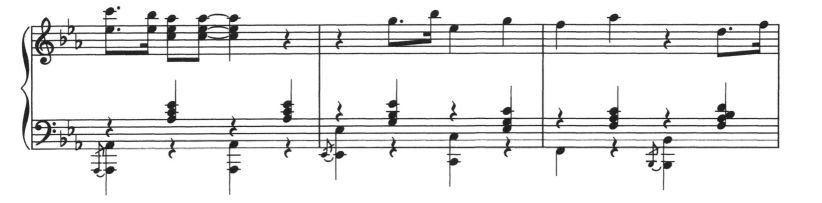

Rudolph, The Red-Nosed Reindeer

Music and Lyrics by
JOHNNY MARKS

Moderately

Moderate Rock

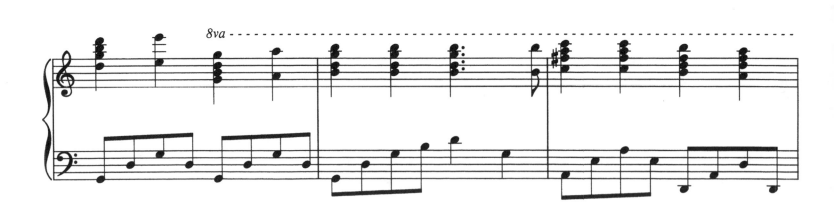

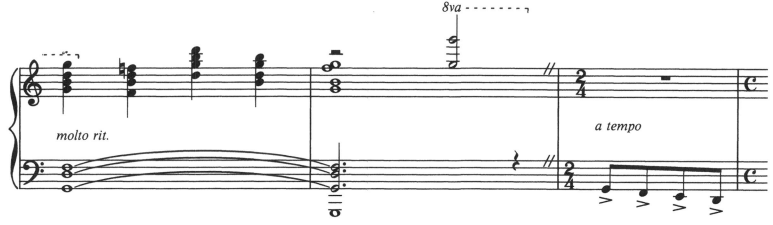

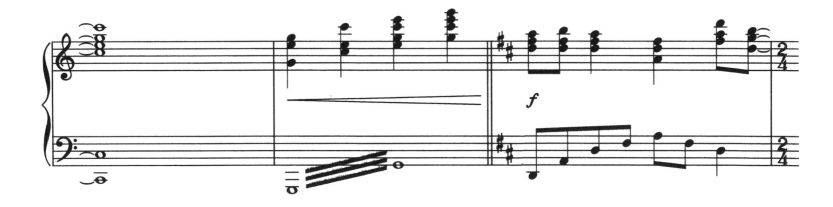

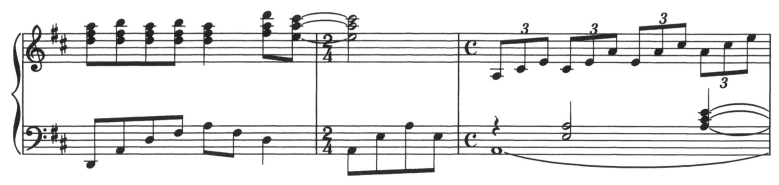

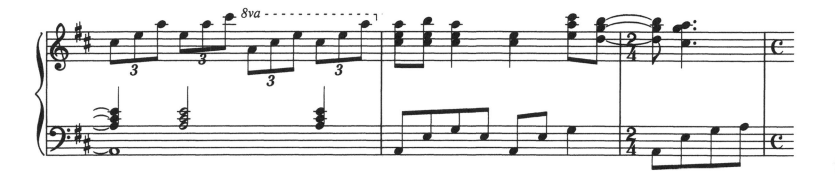

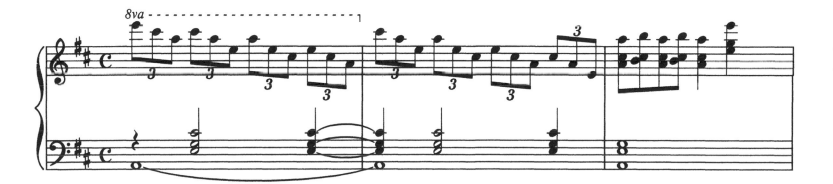

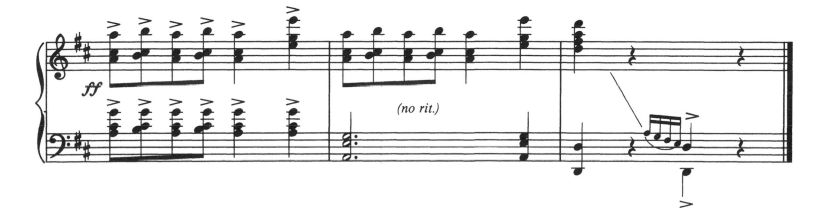

Silver Bells

Moderately with a beat

Words & Music by JAY LIVINGSTON
and RAY EVANS

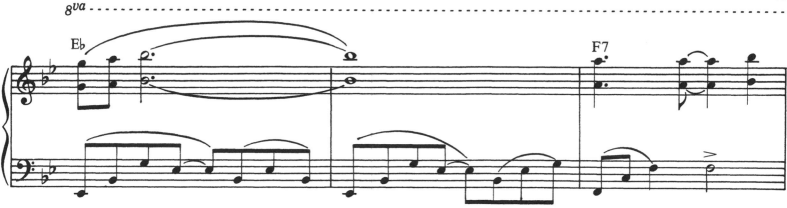

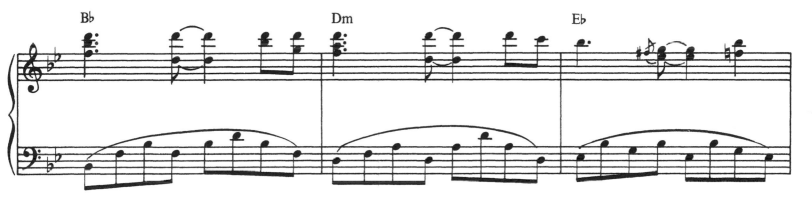

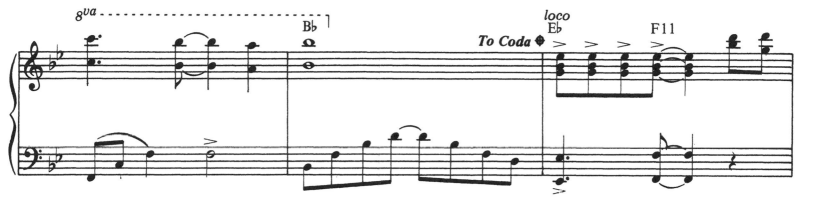

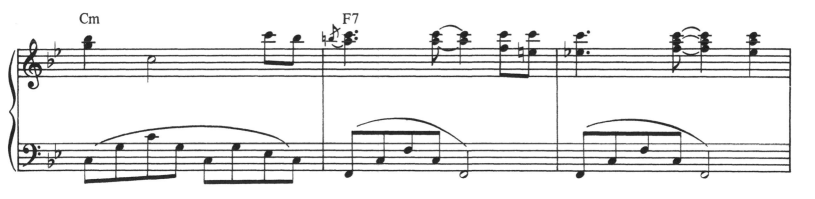

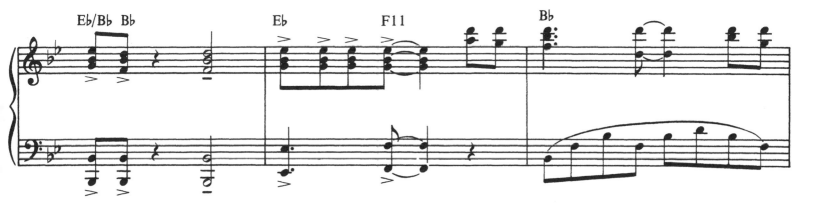

44

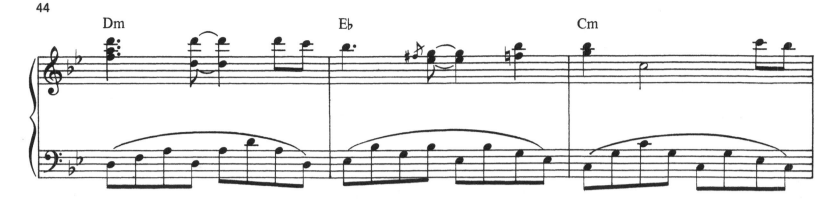

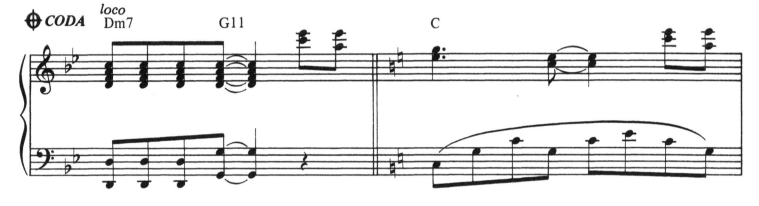

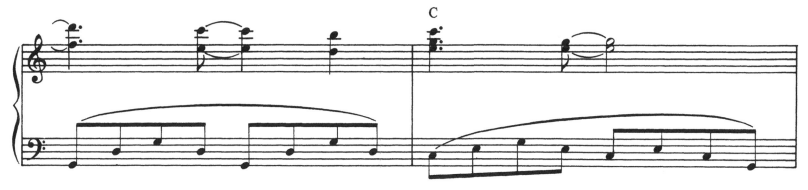

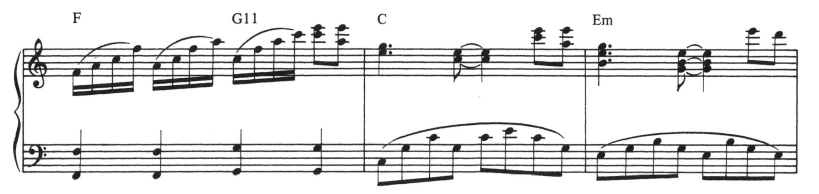

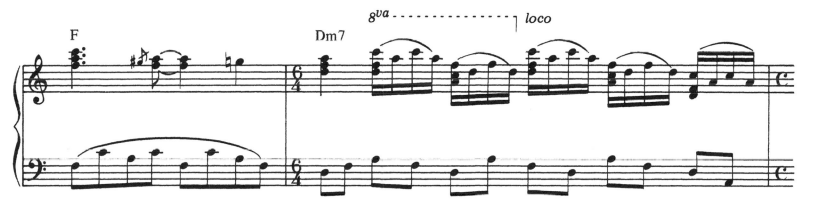

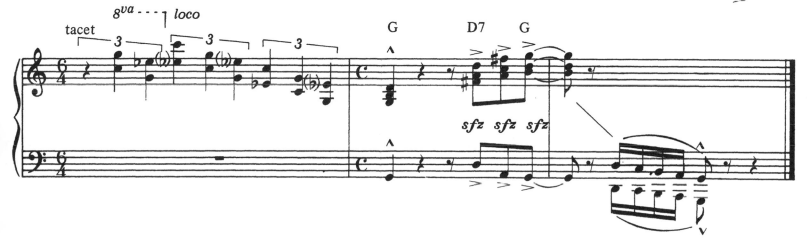

Silent Night - Holy Night

Adaption and Arrangement by OLIVIER TOUSSAINT
and GERARD SALESSES

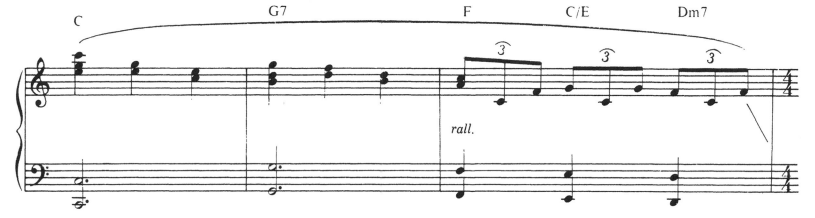

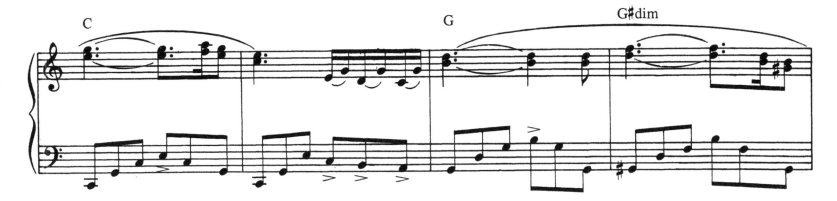

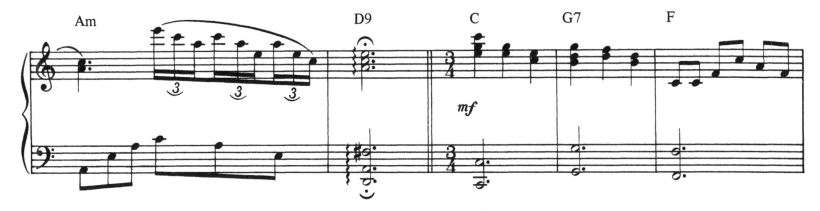